E is for Egg Tart

A Multicultural Alphabet Book

Written By Jessica Lam
Illustrated By Nevy Liang

Dedication

For my sisters, cousins, and every
first-generation kid who grew up
as the only Asian in the class.

Your culture and heritage
are important, too.

Introduction

Once upon a time, not long ago, a little girl was growing up in North Carolina, but she did not feel like she fit in. As a Chinese American, she noticed that her friends did not recognize the foods her family ate or the holidays they celebrated. None of her friends had ever eaten an egg tart, even though it was her favorite food!

Instead of getting discouraged, she sat down and wrote a word for every letter of the alphabet. Each word reflects a part of her culture she wants to share with you and your friends. Do any of these words _sound_ or _look_ familiar to you?

A is for Asian Pear

A fruit that tastes refreshing and sweet –
Hear a big crunch with each bite you eat!

B is for Bok Choy

Layers surround this bright, leafy green –
It makes a nice side, stir-fried or steamed!

C is for Chopsticks

Your fingers work hard to find the right balance –
What a neat skill! Are you up for the challenge?

D is for Drum

It sets a strong beat to gather around –
Listen and feel its big, booming sound!

E is for Egg Tart

A sweet and smooth custard in a hot, flaky crust –
When ordering dim sum, egg tarts are a must!

F is for Fireworks

High in the sky, an explosion of light –
Cover your ears if you don't want a fright!

G is for Ginger

This wrinkly root adds flavor and heat –
A popular spice in all types of treats.

H is for Hot Pot

Everyone gathers to cook and to eat –
What will you choose first:
veggies, seafood, or meat?

I is for Incense

You'll know that it's burning
when the scent hits your nose –
Lit to give thanks and for rituals.

J is for Jade

A precious stone used in jewelry and art –
Often said to bring luck
and worn close to the heart.

K is for Kung Fu

Practice to master your forms and strong stance –
Add swords, staffs, and spears
as you start to advance!

L is for Lychee

A tropical fruit, sweet like no other –
Eat all but the seed!
Will you have another?

M is for Mooncake

A pastry you eat
when the moon is most bright –
Made to be shared on a Mid-Autumn night.

N is for Noodles

Most often made of egg, rice, or flour –
Noodles make a great meal,
no matter the hour!

O is for Oolong

Pour boiling water over the leaves –
If a cup of warm tea
is the drink that you please!

(Sounds like: wu-long, Pinyin: wūlóng)

P is for Panda

Unlike most bears,
pandas are not big on meat –
Chomping bamboo is their favorite treat!

Q is for Qipao

A beautiful dress with high collar and slit –
Often worn by a bride
and made tailored to fit.

(Sounds like: chee-pow, Pinyin: qípáo)

R is for Rice

Scoop each tiny grain into the bowl –
Soaking up sauces,
rice makes a meal whole!

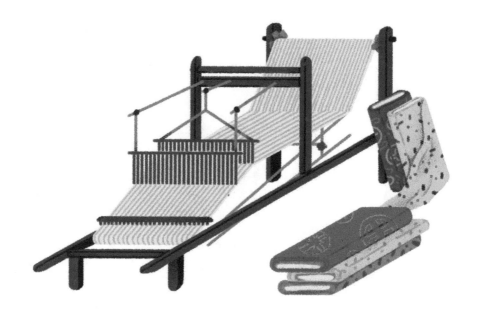

S is for Silk

It's made into fabric that has a soft feel –
But did you know silk
can be stronger than steel?

T is for Temple

Where people can honor traditions or pray –
Expressing belief comes in more than one way.

U is for Umbrella

Used as a cover from rain or the sun –
To escape a big downpour,
you might have to run!

V is for Village

The places where we grow up
are not all the same – In a small village,
neighbors all know your name!

W is for Wok

For tossing and frying and heating up food –
Does it look different
from pans you've seen used?

X is for Xiao Long Bao

These little steamed dumplings
come with a special surprise –
A mouthful of soup in each bite you try!
(Sounds like: shau-long-bau, Pinyin: xiǎolóngbāo)

Y is for Yams

In this family of roots,
there are hundreds of kinds –
From yellow to white to purple inside.

Z is for Zodiac

Every person is different,
but these twelve signs we share –
Let's treat each other with *love* and with *care*!